Fantas

by Emma Glenn

Health

carrot cake

carrots

fruits

lettuce

orange

orange juice

salad

salsa

tomato

vegetables

cauliflower

The *fantastic five* is eating five fruits or vegetables a day.

fruits

mushroom

carrots

These are fruits and vegetables.

Tomatoes can be one of your *fantastic five*.

You can eat a raw tomato.

You can make tomato salsa with tomatoes.

tomato salsa

chilli

tomato

cucumber

The girl has been gathering vegetables and fruits.

Carrots can be one of your *fantastic five*.
You can eat a raw carrot.
You can make carrot cake with carrots.

carrot cake

carrot

basket

These people are
picking carrots.

Oranges can be one of your *fantastic five*.
You can eat an orange
You can make orange juice with oranges.

orange juice

orange

clippers

This man is picking oranges.

Lettuce can be one of your *fantastic five*.
You can make a salad with lettuce and tomatoes.

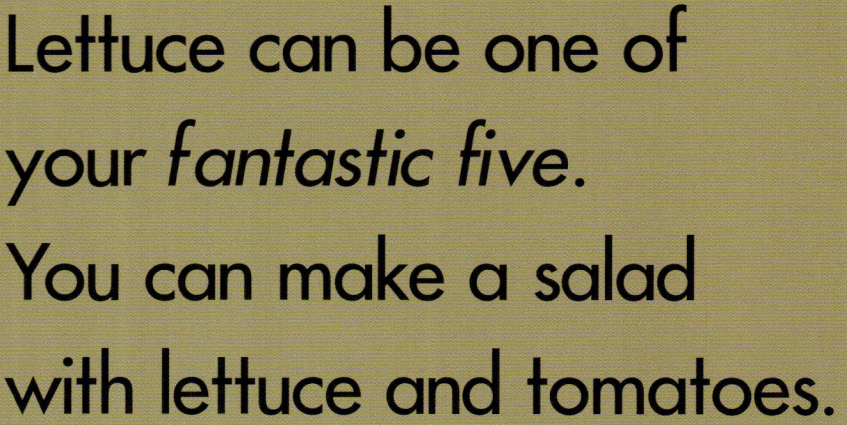

lettuce and tomato salad

cabbage leaf

lettuce

This lady is picking lettuces.

13

Fruits and Vegetables

vegetables

fruits

potato

cabbage

banana

cabbage leaf

cauliflower

clippers

cucumber

watering can